Playing with Plays™ Presents Homer's THE ODYSSEY

FOR KIDS
(The melodramatic version!)

Based off Homer's orignal play
translated by Samuel Butler

For 7-32+ actors, or kids of all ages who want to have fun!
Creatively modified by Amanda Ruby & Brendan P. Kelso
Cover stage illustrated by Shana Hallmeyer
Cover illustrations by Ron Leishman

3 Melodramatic Modifications
for 3 different group sizes:

7-15 actors

14-22 actors

20-32+ actors

Table Of Contents

To my husband, my kids, and my students
for making me want to keep trying
bigger and better things.
-AR

To the Houston OG!
(Jerry, Bridget, Lisa, and Jamie)
Thanks for bringing my plays
to the kids and to life!!!

-BPK

For performance rights please see page 6 of this book or contact:

contact@PlayingWithPlays.com

Foreword

When I was in high school there was something about Shakespeare that appealed to me. Not that I understood it mind you, but there were clear scenes and images that always stood out in my mind. Romeo & Juliet, "Romeo, Romeo; wherefore art thou Romeo?"; Julius Caesar, "Et tu Brute"; Macbeth, "Double, Double, toil and trouble"; Hamlet, "to be or not to be"; A Midsummer Night's Dream, all I remember about this was a wickedly cool fairy and something about a guy turning into a donkey that I thought was pretty funny. It was not until I started analyzing Shakespeare's plays as an actor that I realized one very important thing, I still didn't understand them. Seriously though, it's tough enough for adults, let alone kids. Then it hit me, why don't I make a version that kids could perform, but make it easy for them to understand with a splash of Shakespeare lingo mixed in? And voila! A melodramatic masterpiece was created! They are intended to be melodramatically fun!

THE PLAYS: There are 3 plays within this book, for three different group sizes. The reason: to allow educators or parents to get the story across to their children regardless of the size of their group. As you read through the plays, there are several lines that are highlighted. These are actual lines from the original book. I am a little more particular about the kids saying these lines verbatim. But the rest, well... have fun!

The entire purpose of this book is to instill the love of a classic story, as well as drama, into the kids.

And when you have children who have a passion for something, they will start to teach themselves, with or without school.

These plays are intended for pure fun. Please DO NOT have the kids learn these lines verbatim, that would be a complete waste of creativity. But do have them basically know their lines and improvise wherever they want as long as it pertains to telling the story. Because that is the goal of an actor: to tell the story. In A Midsummer Night's Dream, I once had a student playing Quince question me about one of her lines, "but in the actual story, didn't the Mechanicals state that 'they would hang us'?" I thought for a second and realized that she had read the story with her mom, and she was right. So I let her add the line she wanted and it added that much more fun, it made the play theirs. I have had kids throw water on the audience, run around the audience, sit in the audience, lose their pumpkin pants (size 30 around a size 15 doesn't work very well, but makes for some great humor!) and most importantly, die all over the stage. The kids love it.

One last note: if you want some educational resources, loved our plays, want to tell the world how much your kids loved performing Shakespeare, want to insult someone with our Shakespeare Insult Generator, or are just a fan of Shakespeare, then hop on our website and have fun:

PlayingWithPlays.com

With these notes, I'll see you on the stage, have fun, and break a leg!

SCHOOL, AFTERSCHOOL, and SUMMER classes

I've been teaching these plays as afterschool and summer programs for quite some time. Many people have asked what the program is, therefore, I have put together a basic formula so any teacher or parent can follow and have melodramatic success! As well, many teachers use my books in a variety of ways. You can view the formula and many more resources on my website at: PlayingWithPlays.com

- Brendan

OTHER PLAYS AND FULL LENGTH SCRIPTS

We have over 30 different titles, as well as a full-length play in 4-acts for theatre groups: Shakespeare's Hilarious Tragedies. You can see all of our other titles on our website here: PlayingWithPlays.com/books

As well, you can see a sneak peek at some of those titles at the back of this book.

And, if you ever have any questions, please don't hesitate to ask at: Contact@PlayingWithPlays.com

LICENSES AND ROYALTIES

All performances and other productions require the issuance of a license. Here are the basic guidelines:

1) Please contact us! We always LOVE to hear about a school or group performing our books! We would also love to share photos and brag about your program as well! (with your permission, of course)

2) We require that you purchase a copy of the play for the director/teacher and each kid in the show.

3) If you are a group and DO NOT charge your kids to be in the production, contact us about our educational rates to get a copy in each kid's hands inexpensively. (we will make this work for you!)

4) If you are a group and DO charge your kids to be in the production, (i.e. afterschool program, summer camp), contact us for bulk (10 books or more) or educator's discounts.

5) If you are a group and DO NOT charge the audience to see the plays, please see our website FAQs (www.PlayingWithPlays.com) to see if you are eligible to waive the performance license(s) (most performances are eligible).

6) If you are a group and DO charge the audience to see the performance, please see our website FAQs for performance licensing fees (this includes performances for donations and competitions).

Any other questions or comments, please see our website or email us at:

contact@PlayingWithPlays.com

The 15-Minute or so
THE ODYSSEY
for Kids
by Homer
Creatively modified by
Amanda Ruby & Brendan P. Kelso
7-15 Actors

CAST OF CHARACTERS:

[7]**ODYSSEUS**: our hero, on a long work trip

[7]**YOUNG ODYSSEUS**: our hero, but younger

[3]**PENELOPE**: his smart wife

[6]**CREW 1**: member of Odysseus's crew

[6]**CREW 2**: member of Odysseus's crew

[1]**CYCLOPS**: a hideous beast with one eye (for now)

[5]**CIRCE**: a lady who loves animals

[4]**HERMES**: mischievous Greek god and messenger

[4]**SIREN 1**: a deadly singer

[5]**SIREN 2**: another deadly singer

[2]**CALYPSO**: wants to marry Odysseus

[3]**POSEIDON**: Greek god of the sea

[4]**SUITOR**: wants to marry Penelope

[2]**ANTINOUS**: the worst suitor (also, wants Penelope)

[1]**COW**: it's a cow or lunch, depends on your perspective

SCYLLA: Nonspeaking, 6 headed monster - offstage

Extras can play townspeople, crew members, suitors, sirens all these parts have no lines, but you can add some if you like!

The same actors can play the following parts:

[1]CYCLOPES and COW
[2]CALYPSO and ANTINOUS
[3]PENELOPE and POSEIDON
[4]HERMES, SIREN, and SUITOR
[5]CIRCE and SIREN
[6]CREW 1 and 2 - HOWEVER - some lines will need to be modified at director's discretion.
[7]ODYSSEUS and YOUNG ODYSSEUS - HOWEVER - some lines will need to be modified at director's discretion.

ACT 1 SCENE 1
Odysseus is Home

(PENELOPE and ODYSSEUS run toward each other)

ODYSSEUS: Penelope! I'm home!

PENELOPE: Finally! By the way, Odysseus, where have you been these past TWO DECADES?

ODYSSEUS: Ummm... nowhere?

PENELOPE: Hmmm, nice try. Cough it up.

ODYSSEUS: Well, okay.

(YOUNG ODYSSEUS and CREW enter rowing)

ACT 1 SCENE 2

The Cyclops

ODYSSEUS: *(to audience)* Once upon a time, on the way home from the great Trojan War, a hurricane pushed us off course. *(ODYSSEUS sees YOUNG ODYSSEUS)* Aww, look how young I looked!

(YOUNG ODYSSEUS clears throat)

ODYSSEUS: Sorry, go ahead.

CREW 1: We've been rowing for months!

CREW 2: Look! Land!

CREW 1: It's full of flowers!

CREW 2: And the people look SOOOO happy!

YOUNG ODYSSEUS: NO. No, no, no, no! My buddy Jack has been there for decades, just eating flowers and staring at a wall. We are NOT stopping there!

CREW: Awwww. *(continue rowing)*

ODYSSEUS: We sailed until we came to the land of the Cyclops. *(enter CYCLOPS)* He was a horrid creature, not like a human being at all!

CYCLOPS: I resent that.

ODYSSEUS: No. RESEMBLE is the word you're looking for. *(CYCLOPS glares)* He stuck us in a cave, grabbed my crew, and ate them. *(CYCLOPS eats CREW 1 and 2, they die)*

CREW 1 & 2: Hey!

PENELOPE: He. Ate. Them? *(retches)*

ODYSSEUS: Yeah.

CYCLOPS: In my defense, I was hungry, and they are delicious. *(burps)* Sorry. Continue.

YOUNG ODYSSEUS: You ought to be ashamed of yourself.

CYCLOPS: I know, but I don't get many visitors.

YOUNG ODYSSEUS: That's because you eat them!

CYCLOPS: That's true.

YOUNG ODYSSEUS: Please, drink this juice.

CYCLOPS: Don't mind if I do. Cheers. *(drinks)* That is good. More, please!

ODYSSEUS: And I gave him more. Lots more!

CYCLOPS: *(to audience)* I will eat all of Noman's crew! But I will save Noman for last. He looks tasty! *(yawns)* Wow, this juice makes me sleepy.

ODYSSEUS: As he spoke, he fell to the ground. I blinded him!

CYCLOPS: Do you have to?

YOUNG ODYSSEUS: Yeah, I do.

CYCLOPS: Well, if you must.

YOUNG ODYSSEUS: I must. *(blinds CYCLOPES)*

CYCLOPS: Ahhhh! My eye!!! *(stumbles around)*

ODYSSEUS: Then we escaped.

PENELOPE: You are crafty.

ODYSSEUS: Yes. Yes, I am.

CYCLOPS: I'll get you! *(tries to grab YOUNG ODYSSEUS)*

YOUNG ODYSSEUS: *(dodges CYCLOPS)* Neener, neener, boo, boo! *(sticks tongue at CYCLOPS)*

PENELOPE: Now, you're being just mean.

ODYSSEUS: Really? He ate six of my crew. Six!

CREW: Yeah!

PENELOPE: Fine.

CYCLOPS: I'm telling my dad! *(exits)*

ODYSSEUS: Unfortunately, his dad was Poseidon, God of the sea.

PENELOPE: His dad was Poseidon?! NOW, I'm starting to undestand why it took you 20 years!

(ALL exit)

ACT 1 SCENE 3

Circe

(PENELOPE and CREW enter)

CREW 1: We arrived at the Aeolian Island.

PENELOPE: Wait a minute. Who are you? Didn't you just get eaten?

CREW 1: Who, me? No. Maybe... I have no idea what you're talking about.

PENELOPE: *(suspicious)* Okay... go on.

CREW 2: Before we left, the Aeolian king gave Odysseus a bag of wind.

PENELOPE: A bag of what?

CREW 2: Wind! See! *(holds up bag)* It holds the bad winds so we could sail home safely.

CREW 1: Can I hold it?!

CREW 2: Sure! *(CREW 1 runs around the stage playing with it)*

PENELOPE: Well, that's good!

CREW 2: It was, until Odysseus took a nap.

PENELOPE: What happened?

CREW 2: Some curious crew member, NOT ME, *(looks sternly at CREW 1)* opened the bag and the wind flew howling forth and raised a storm that carried us back out to sea.

(CREW 1 opens bag and ALL get blown around stage)

YOUNG ODYSSEUS: *(enters stretching)* What is happening here? *(ALL stop)* Why aren't we on shore yet?

CREW 2: About that...

(points at CREW 1)

CREW 1: Sorry boss.

YOUNG ODYSSEUS: What?! You're first to be eaten next time!

CREW 1: Okay. Next time?

ODYSSEUS: *(enters)* So, we sailed on until we came to the island where Circe lives.

YOUNG ODYSSEUS: Look up ahead. I see a house!

CREW 1: I think I'll just stay here on the ship.

CREW 2: Oh, come on, you big baby!

CREW 1: I don't want to be eaten again.

YOUNG ODYSSEUS: Yeah, don't be a baby. You go and I'LL stay with the ship. *(stands to side)*

CREW 1: Aw, man!

(CREW walks around stage)

CIRCE: *(enters singing)* Why, hello strangers! Come on in! I'll get you some cookies!

CREW 2: Yes! Cookies!!!

(CREW chants "cookies, cookies, cookies...")

CREW 2: *(to audience)* But the food was enchanted, and we turned into pigs.

PENELOPE: Pigs? Really?

CREW 2: Yes, really. Oink!

(CREW starts acting like pigs)

CIRCE: Here you go, little piggies! *(tosses treats to pigs)*

CREW 1: This is HOGwash!

CREW 2: Oh, are we doing jokes? What's my pig name? *(CREW shrugs)* Chris P. Bacon!

CREW 1: Ugh. Enough. This is humiliating. Oink.

CIRCE: Come on little piggies. We're off to market!

(CIRCE and CREW exit)

ODYSSEUS: The god Hermes saw what happened and decided to help. After, he laughed at us.

(HERMES enters; laughing)

HERMES: God of deliveries here!

YOUNG ODYSSEUS: Hermes! I'd love to chat, but Circe turned my crew into pigs and I must save them.

HERMES: Take this herb.

YOUNG ODYSSEUS: Okay. Thanks?

HERMES: Eat it.

YOUNG ODYSSEUS: All right. Pushy-pushy. Mmmm, tasty.

HERMES: The herb will stop the pig spell from working.

YOUNG ODYSSEUS: Ahhh! Good!

HERMES: Also, after she falls in love with you, ask her to change your crew back.

PENELOPE: Excuse me. After she what?! *(she's ignored)*

YOUNG ODYSSEUS: Sure. Can I go now?

PENELOPE: Hello?! *(stomps foot, still ignored; upset off to side)*

HERMES: Fine. YOU'RE WELCOME, by the way. *(to audience)* No one appreciates the messenger. Humph. *(exits)*

YOUNG ODYSSEUS: *(yells)* Circe! I've come to save my crew!

CIRCE: *(enters with cookie)* Odysseus! Perfect timing! Cookie?

YOUNG ODYSSEUS: I love cookies! *(eats)*

CIRCE: Wait, why aren't you a pig?

YOUNG ODYSSEUS: Because I've got a magic herb to protect me!

CIRCE: Drat. You know, you're kind of cute.

PENELOPE: That's it!! *(approaches CIRCE)*

YOUNG ODYSSEUS: *(holds PENELOPE back)* Let ME handle this. *(draws sword)* Un-pig my crew!

CIRCE: Anything for you... darling. *(snaps fingers and CREW enters no longer pigs)*

CREW 1: Oh man, I think I ate garbage.

CREW 2: Oh! I've got another one! What's a pig's favorite play? HAMlet! *(CREW groans)* No, HAMalot. *(CREW groans louder)* Dear Evan HAMson? *(CREW really annoyed)*. HAMilton!!!

CREW 1: *(to CREW 2)* No. PLEASE, make it stop.

CREW 2: Fine! *(to audience)* We stayed with Circe for a year...

PENELOPE: WHAT!?!?!

ODYSSEUS: *(shrugs)* She made really good cookies!

CREW 2: Odysseus, it is time you began to think about going home.

YOUNG ODYSSEUS: Yeah, you're probably right. Circe, thanks for the hospitality, but we should be going.

CIRCE: Fine. You can leave.

PENELOPE: About time. *(CIRCE and PENELOPE glare at each other)*

CIRCE: But first, you must go to Hades to consult the blind prophet Teiresias.

YOUNG ODYSSEUS: Do we have to? Prophets are soooo depressing.

CIRCE: Yes. Teiresias will tell you what you must do to get home.

YOUNG ODYSSEUS: *(sigh)* Okay. Crew, we're off to Hades!

CREW: AWWWWW!

CIRCE: Bye, bye, little piggies! *(oinks)*

(ALL but YOUNG ODYSSES exit)

ACT 1 SCENE 4
Sirens and Scylla

(YOUNG ODYSSEUS enters)

YOUNG ODYSSEUS: *(to audience)* So, I just returned from the underworld. We have quite the adventures ahead. Unfortunatly, all my crew doesn't make it... actually, none of them do.

(CREW enters)

CREW 1: How was the meeting with Hade's prophet?

YOUNG ODYSSEUS: Ummm... excellent. I'm going to make it home!

CREW 2: And us?

YOUNG ODYSSEUS: Oh, look! Danger! *(points offstage)*

CREW 1: We soon came upon the first of many dangers.

YOUNG ODYSSEUS: Okay, here come the Sirens. Take this wax and stuff it in your ears. Now, tie me up!

CREW 2: What?

YOUNG ODYSSEUS: TIE ME UP! You won't hear the Siren's song because of the wax. But I want to be the first to hear it and live. Apparently, it's a catchy tune!

(CREW ties him up, starts speaking loudly)

CREW 1: You know, I'm not so sure this job was worth it.

CREW 2: I know, cannibals, pigs, monsters, now this!

CREW 1: Yeah, Odysseus is strange.

YOUNG ODYSSEUS: I heard that!

CREW 1: Oh, sorry!

(CREW starts rowing; SIRENS enter, say lines sing-song)

SIREN 1: Oh, brave Odysseus.

SIREN 2: Hero of men.

SIREN 1: Come to us...

SIREN 2: And never leave again! *(ALL laugh evilly)*

YOUNG ODYSSEUS: Okay, you can untie me now.

(CREW looks confused, can't hear him; YOUNG ODYSSEUS mimes untying)

CREW 2: Oh, sure thing, captain!

CREW 1: NO! He'll take us straight to the Sirens and they will eat us all!

YOUNG ODYSSEUS: They can't possibly eat ALL of us. I'm sure I'LL be okay!

CREW 2: Sorry, boss!

SIREN 1: Come closer to us...

SIREN 2: Your future will reveal...

SIREN 1: Secrets no man knows...

SIREN 2: *(to SIREN 1)* Odysseus will make a nice meal!

YOUNG ODYSSEUS: Untie me or else!!!

CREW 1: The captain looks mad!

CREW 2: Row faster!

SIRENS: *(SIRENS turn angry and reach for the ship)* NOOO! You mustn't escape!

CREW 1: This isn't the first time that we have been in danger! ROW!

(*CREW rows furiously*)

SIRENS: NOOOOOOOOOOOOOOOOOOOOO!!! (*exit melodramatically*)

YOUNG ODYSSEUS: (*to the audience*) We sailed out of earshot and the crew untied me.

CREW 2: Whew. Glad that's over.

ODYSSEUS: (*enters, to audience*) Then Scylla, a 6-headed monster, pounced down and snatched up two of my crew.

(*arms reach through the curtains and snatch CREW backstage*)

CREW 1: WHAT IS HAPPENING?!?

(*screaming backstage*)

CREW 2: (*enters to YOUNG ODYSSEUS*) Did you know that was going to happen?

YOUNG ODYSSEUS: Uh... no? Keep rowing! We're almost past her.

CREW 1: (*enters*) That was terrible.

CREW 2: (*enters*) Yeah, that's the third time I've died in this show!

(*CREW rows*)

ACT 1 SCENE 6
Forbidden Cows

CREW 1: Look! Land!

YOUNG ODYSSEUS: Oh! I almost forgot; we can't stop here!

CREW: WHAT?!

YOUNG ODYSSEUS: It is the most dangerous place yet. Keep going!

CREW 1: They're just a bunch of cows, boss.

CREW 2: Maybe they are mutant cows that will eat us.

CREW 1: I'm tired of being eaten. I need to rest.

CREW 2: Me too!

CREW 1: Come on, sir. Let us stop.

YOUNG ODYSSEUS: Alright. Alright. But, you MUST promise not to harm a single cow.

CREW: Promise!

ODYSSEUS: *(to audience)* We came ashore and fell fast asleep. But, during the night, Zeus raised a great gale of wind, causing a hurricane.

CREW 1: Looks like we are stuck here.

YOUNG ODYSSEUS: We have lots of food on the ship. Remember, do NOT kill any cows!

CREW: Yes, sir! No cows!

ODYSSEUS: The hurricane blew for an entire month...

ALL: A MONTH!?!?

ODYSSEUS: We ran out of food. The days were long. I left my crew to take a nap. *(YOUNG ODYSSEUS exits)*

CREW 2: He naps at the strangest times.

CREW 1: I've never been this hungry in my life.

(COW enters)

COW: Moo.

CREW 2: Look! There's a nice, juicy hamburger. I-I-I mean cow.

COW: Moo?

CREW 1: Let's get it!

COW: Moo!!!

(CREW chases COW offstage, moo sounds from backstage, CREW enters licking their lips carrying "hamburger" supplies)

CREW 2: Now that hit the spot.

YOUNG ODYSSEUS: *(enters; sees hamburger paraphernalia)* Come on! I told you ONE thing. DO NOT eat the cows!

CREW 1: Sorry, boss. But it was only one.

CREW 2: And it was DELICIOUS!

CREW 1: Finally, the wind died down, and we set sail with full bellies!

(CREW rows)

CREW 2: As soon as we were away from the island, a black cloud formed over our ship.

CREW 1: *(points offstage)* It's Zeus!!!

(stirs up a storm, ALL blow around stage)

YOUNG ODYSSEUS: He's mad you ate the cow!!! I told you so!

ODYSSEUS: *(to audience)* Zeus let fly his thunderbolts, the ship caught on fire, and the crew fell into the sea.

CREW 1: I guess this is it for us. Nice knowing you!

CREW 2: That burger was worth it!!!

(CREW exits screaming)

ACT 2 SCENE 1

The Gods Interfere

(PENELOPE enters)

PENELOPE: Are you STILL telling this story?

ODYSSEUS: Hey, it was 20 years! *(to audience)* So, I floated to the Island of Calypso.

PENELOPE: She was nice and helped you?

ODYSSEUS: She captured me and held me in a cave.

CALYPSO: *(enters)* What? Can't a girl keep a guy in a cave until he agrees to marry her?!

PENELOPE: *(to CALYPSO)* I didn't have to capture him to get him to marry ME.

CALYPSO: *(shrugs)* Whatever. *(to YOUNG ODYSSEUS)* Let's go... prisoner.

(CALYPSO and YOUNG ODYSSEUS exit opposite PENELOPE and ODYSSEUS)

HERMES: *(enters)* But, as the years went by, the gods decided it was time for Odysseus to go home. And when I say the gods, I mean Zeus.

ACT 2 SCENE 2
Calypso

HERMES: Hello? Calypso?

CALYPSO: *(enters)* Oh, hello Hermes. What are YOU doing here?

HERMES: Nice place ya got here. Zeus sent me.

CALYPSO: Okaaaaay.

HERMES: Zeus says you must let Odysseus go.

CALYPSO: Really? *(full of rage)* Aghhhh! You gods ought to be ashamed of yourselves! You're just mad a goddess is in love with a mortal man!

HERMES: Hey, don't kill the messenger! Literally. Don't. Well, you can't anyway. Gods are immortal! Ha, ha!

CALYPSO: ARGH!

HERMES: Anyway, you know what happens if you say no to the big guy.

(HERMES makes a slit throat motion)

CALYPSO: FINE! I'll send him away.

HERMES: Great! I'm out of here! *(exits)*

CALYPSO: *(calls offstage)* Odysseus! Come here, darling!

ODYSSEUS: *(enters, sad)* What now?

CALYPSO: I'm sending you away. You can make yourself a raft. Don't be too sad, darling. Zeus insists it be so.

ODYSSEUS: YIPPEE!

CALYPSO: DON'T BE TOO SAD, DARLING!

ODYSSEUS: Oh, I mean, bummer. But a raft? I don't know if that's a good idea. You know, Poseidon.

CALYPSO: Well, if you want to stay...

ODYSSEUS: No! No, no. Raft is good!

CALYPSO: Oh well. Easy come, easy go. *(exits)*

ODYSSEUS: Off I sailed, until, of course, Poseidon noticed me.

POSEIDON: *(enters)* Who's that there? Is that Odysseus? He thinks he can just float home after blinding MY son!

ODYSSEUS: Poseidon gathered his clouds together, grasped his trident, stirred it around the sea, and roused the rage of every wind that blows.

POSEIDON: Oh yeah, I did! Winds from every direction hit Odysseus and his silly little raft all at once!

(POSEIDON making magical gestures while ODYSSEUS mimes thrashing in ocean)

ODYSSEUS: I was thrown from the raft into the crashing waves.

POSEIDON: Ha! Take that!

ODYSSEUS: But I was able to swim back and climb on.

POSEIDON: REALLY?!?

ODYSSEUS: Poseidon sent a terrible great wave and destroyed my raft.

POSEIDON: Take that!

ODYSSEUS: Then, I got on a plank of wood.

POSEIDON: This guy never dies! I give up. *(exits)*

ODYSSEUS: I floated until I made it to shore. Long story short...

ALL BACKSTAGE: Too late!

ACT 2 SCENE 3

Odysseus Returns

ODYSSEUS: I finally made it home! I went to my house as a beggar. *(changes outfit)*

(PENELOPE, ANTINOUS, and SUITOR enter)

PENELOPE: *(to the suitors)* Listen up, boys. I have a great idea! This is the bow of Odysseus. Whomsoever of you shall string, and send his arrow through each one of twelve axes, I will marry.

(SUITORS cheer)

SUITOR: *(trying to string bow and failing miserably)* Ugh. This is too hard. Next!

ANTINOUS: Give me that! *(struggles)* This bow is impossible. Let's just forget this ever happened.

(SUITOR agrees)

ODYSSEUS: I'd like to try it.

ANTINOUS: You?!? Keep quiet without getting into a quarrel with men younger than yourself.

(SUITOR cheers in agreement)

PENELOPE: ENOUGH! Are you afraid he will make you all look like fools?

ODYSSEUS: Don't upset yourself, Penelope. Let me see that bow. Oh, and you may want to go backstage for this next part. It's a bit gruesome.

(PENELOPE exits; ODYSSEUS takes the bow and strings it, then shoots an arrow off-stage; SUITORS are awestruck)

ACT 2 Scene 4

The Suitors' Demise

ODYSSEUS: Dogs, did you think that I should not come back? You ate my food, mistreated my servants, and wooed my wife. You have feared neither God nor man, and now you shall die.

SUITOR: It's Odysseus! Scatter!

(SUITORS run around screaming)

ODYSSEUS: Antinous!

ANTINOUS: Who me?

(ODYSSEUS kills ANTINOUS; SUITOR sees ANTINOUS, then screams)

SUITOR: Have mercy!

ODYSSEUS: Let me think about it. Nope. *(to audience)* Since this part is a bit gruesome, we will skip it. But to summarize, they all died. *(snaps fingers, suitor falls dead)*

PENELOPE: *(enters)* Hello stranger. A mighty big pile of bodies you've got there. You're really embracing the ol' epic Greek tragedy, aren't you?

ODYSSEUS: Exactly. An epic story must have an EPIC ending. And THIS is the original epic story. Wife, it is me, Odysseus! *(sheds costume)*

PENELOPE: *(running towards ODYSSEUS in slow motion)* O-dyss-e-us!

ODYSSEUS: Pe-nel-o-pe! *(running towards PENELOPE in slow motion)*

PENELOPE: And we all lived happily ever after.

ANTINOUS: Um, excuse me? Does this look happy?

SUITOR: We just got slaughtered, remember?

ODYSSEUS: Ugh, that was several lines ago, get over it.

(SUITORS die again)

PENELOPE: As I said, HAPPILY EVER AFTER!

THE END

The 20-Minute or so
THE ODYSSEY
for Kids

by Homer
Creatively modified by
Amanda Ruby & Brendan P. Kelso
14-22 Actors

CAST OF CHARACTERS:

ODYSSEUS: our hero, on a long work trip
YOUNG ODYSSEUS: our hero, but younger
PENELOPE: his smart wife
TELEMACHUS: their son
CREW 1: member of Odysseus's crew
CREW 2: member of Odysseus's crew
CREW 3: member of Odysseus's crew
CREW 4: member of Odysseus's crew
[1]**CYCLOPS:** a hideous beast with one eye (for now)
[4]**TOWNSPERSON:** someone who lives in town
[3]**OGRE:** likes to eat people and smash things
[6]**CIRCE:** a lady who loves animals
[5]**HERMES:** mischievous Greek god and messenger
[5]**SIREN 1:** a deadly singer
[6]**SIREN 2:** another deadly singer
[4]**ZEUS:** Greek god of the sky - the big guy
[2]**CALYPSO:** wants to marry Odysseus
[3]**POSEIDON:** Greek god of the sea
[5]**SUITOR 1:** wants to marry Penelope

⁶SUITOR 2: also, wants to marry Penelope
²ANTINOUS: the worst suitor (also, wants Penelope)
¹COW: it's a cow, or lunch, depends on your perspective
SCYLLA: Nonspeaking, 6 headed monster - offstage
Extras can play townspeople, crew members, suitors, sirens all these parts have no lines, but you can add some if you like!

The same actors can play the following parts:

¹CYCLOPES and COW
²CALYPSO and ANTINOUS
³OGRE and POSEIDON
⁴TOWNSPERSON and ZEUS
⁵HERMES, SIREN, and SUITOR
⁶CIRCE, SIREN, and SUITOR

ACT 1 SCENE 1
Odysseus is Home

(PENELOPE and ODYSSEUS run toward each other, TELEMACHUS follows)

ODYSSEUS: Penelope! I'm home!

PENELOPE: Finally! Odysseus, this is your son, Telemachus.

ODYSSEUS: *(baby talk)* Daddy missed you!

TELEMACHUS: Ahh, yeah, you've been gone, like, 20 years. Not quite a baby anymore.

ODYSSEUS: Oh, right... dude! *(awkward high-five; TELEMACHUS rolls eyes)*

PENELOPE: *(to audience)* And we all lived happily ever after. *(ODYSSEUS and PENELOPE bow)*

TELEMACHUS: Wait, what? We literally just started. These people came to see a play. *(to audience)* Right? *(gets audience to cheer)*

ALL: *(everyone thinks)* Hmmm.

PENELOPE: Well... Odysseus, you could tell us what you've been doing these past TWO DECADES.

ODYSSEUS: Ummm... nothing?

PENELOPE: Hmmm, nice try. Cough it up.

ODYSSEUS: Well, okay.

(YOUNG ODYSSEUS and CREW enter rowing)

ACT 1 SCENE 2

The Cyclops

ODYSSEUS: *(to audience)* Once upon a time, on the way home from the great Trojan War, a hurricane pushed us off course. *(ODYSSEUS sees YOUNG ODYSSEUS)* Aww, look how young I looked!

(YOUNG ODYSSEUS clears throat)

ODYSSEUS: Sorry, go ahead.

CREW 1: We've been rowing for months!

CREW 2: Look! Land!

CREW 3: It's full of flowers!

CREW 4: And the people look SOOOO happy!

YOUNG ODYSSEUS: NO. No, no, no, no! My buddy Jack has been there for decades, just eating flowers and staring at a wall. We are NOT stopping there!

CREW: Awwww. *(continue rowing)*

ODYSSEUS: We sailed until we came to the land of the Cyclops. *(enter CYCLOPS)* He was a horrid creature, not like a human being at all!

CYCLOPS: I resent that.

ODYSSEUS: No. RESEMBLE is the word you're looking for. *(CYCLOPS glares)* He stuck us in a cave, grabbed two of my crew, and ate them. *(CYCLOPS eats CREW 1 and 2, they die)*

CREW 1 & 2: Hey!

PENELOPE: He. Ate. Them? *(retches)*

ODYSSEUS: Yeah.

CYCLOPS: In my defense, I was hungry.

ODYSSEUS: Then he ate two more! *(eats 3 and 4, they die)*

CYCLOPS: *(burps)* Sorry. Continue.

YOUNG ODYSSEUS: You ought to be ashamed of yourself.

CYCLOPS: I know, but I don't get many visitors.

YOUNG ODYSSEUS: That's because you eat them!

CYCLOPS: That's true. What's your name?

YOUNG ODYSSEUS: My name is Noman. Please, drink this juice.

CYCLOPS: Don't mind if I do. Cheers. *(drinks)* That is good. More, please!

ODYSSEUS: And I gave him more. Lots more!

CYCLOPS: *(to audience)* I will eat all of Noman's crew! But I will save Noman for last. He looks tasty! *(yawns)* Wow, this juice makes me sleepy.

ODYSSEUS: As he spoke, he fell to the ground. I blinded him!

CYCLOPS: Do you have to?

YOUNG ODYSSEUS: Yeah, I do.

CYCLOPS: Well, if you must.

YOUNG ODYSSEUS: I must. *(blinds CYCLOPES)*

CYCLOPS: Ahhhh! My eye!!! *(stumbles around)*

ODYSSEUS: Cyclops made such a ruckus the townspeople came.

TOWNSPERSON: *(enters)* What's going on? Surely no man is trying to kill YOU!

CYCLOPS: *("no-man")* Noman is killing me! Noman is killing me!

TOWNSPERSON: Well, if no man is killing you, keep it down. People are trying to sleep! *(exits)*

ODYSSEUS: Then we escaped.

TELEMACHUS: You are crafty.

ODYSSEUS: Yes. Yes, I am.

CYCLOPS: I'll get you! *(tries to grab YOUNG ODYSSEUS)*

YOUNG ODYSSEUS: *(dodges CYCLOPS)* Neener, neener, boo, boo! *(sticks tongue at CYCLOPS)*

PENELOPE: Now, you're being just mean.

ODYSSEUS: Really? He ate six of my crew. Six!

CREW: Yeah!

PENELOPE: Fine.

YOUNG ODYSSEUS: *(to CYCLOPS)* Also, my real name is Odysseus! Ha, ha!!!

CYCLOPS: I'm telling my dad! *(exits)*

ODYSSEUS: Unfortunately, his dad was Poseidon, God of the sea.

TELEMACHUS: His dad was Poseidon?! Dude, you are so ruined!

ODYSSEUS & YOUNG ODYSSEUS: Right?!

(ALL exit)

ACT 1 SCENE 3
Circe

(PENELOPE, TELEMACHAUS, and CREW enter)

CREW 4: We arrived at the Aeolian Island.

PENELOPE: Wait a minute. Who are you? Didn't you just get eaten?

CREW 4: Who, me? No. Maybe... I have no idea what you're talking about.

PENELOPE: *(suspicious)* Okay... go on.

CREW 4: Before we left, the Aeolian king gave Odysseus a bag of wind.

PENELOPE: A bag of what?

CREW 2: Wind! See! *(holds up bag)* It holds the bad winds so we could sail home safely.

CREW 3: Can I hold it?!

CREW 2: Sure! *(CREW 3 runs around the stage playing with it)*

PENELOPE: Well, that's good!

CREW 1: It was, until Odysseus took a nap.

TELEMACHUS: What happened?

CREW 4: Some curious crew member, NOT ME, *(ALL CREW look sternly at CREW 3)* opened the bag and the wind flew howling forth and raised a storm that carried us back out to sea.

(CREW 3 opens bag and ALL get blown around stage)

YOUNG ODYSSEUS: *(enters stretching)* What is happening here? *(ALL stop)* Why aren't we on shore yet?

CREW 1: About that...

(ALL CREW point to CREW 3)

CREW 3: Sorry boss.

YOUNG ODYSSEUS: What?! You're first to be eaten next time!

CREW 3: Okay. Next time?

ODYSSEUS: *(enters)* So, we sailed on until we reached the city of the Laestrygonians.

(CREW rows)

PENELOPE: OK, and then?

ODYSSEUS: Then ogres! They're giants and cannibals.

TELEMACHUS: Wasn't the Cyclops a giant and a cannibal?

ODYSSEUS: Yes, but he had one eye and was the son of a god.

TELEMACHUS: Oh. Right. Totally different. Go on.

YOUNG ODYSSEUS: Okay, crew, let's stop here and rest.

CREW 2: Aye, aye, captain.

CREW 1: *(to audience)* Oh, look! An ogre!

(OGRE enters)

OGRE: Yay! I get to eat and crush.

(YOUNG ODYSSEUS refers to CREW 3)

YOUNG ODYSSEUS: Yo, you're up.

CREW 3: I get eaten again?! *(gets eaten)*

YOUNG ODYSSEUS: Told you!

CREW 4: Oh, goody! This time I get crushed by a boulder, instead of eaten! *(gets crushed)*

OGRE: *(to audience)* I love my job. I'm going to throw boulders at their ships and sink them. Then I'll take a nap. Eating humans makes me sleepy.

(OGRE exits, CREW rises, rowing)

CREW 2: *(to audience)* We escaped to our one hidden ship and sailed on until we came to the island where Circe lives.

YOUNG ODYSSEUS: Look up ahead. I see a house!

CREW 3: I think I'll just stay here on the ship.

CREW 4: Oh, come on, you big baby!

YOUNG ODYSSEUS: Yeah, don't be a baby. You go and I'LL stay with the ship. *(stands to side)*

CREW 3: Aw, man!

(CREW walks around stage)

CIRCE: *(enters singing)* Why, hello strangers! Come on in! I'll get you some cookies!

CREW 2: Yes! Cookies!!!

(CREW chants "cookies, cookies, cookies...")

CREW 1: *(to audience)* But the food was enchanted, and we turned into pigs.

TELEMACHUS: Pigs? Really?

CREW 1: Yes, really. Oink!

(CREW starts acting like pigs)

CIRCE: Here you go, little piggies! *(tosses treats to pigs)*

CREW 1: This is HOGwash!

CREW 3: Yeah, what is this place, HOGwarts?

CREW 2: Oh, are we doing jokes? What's my pig name? *(CREW shrugs)* Chris P. Bacon!

CREW 1: Ugh. Enough. This is humiliating. Oink.

CIRCE: Come on little piggies. We're off to market!

(CIRCE and CREW exit)

ODYSSEUS: The god Hermes saw what happened and decided to help. After, he laughed at us.

(HERMES enters; laughing)

HERMES: God of deliveries here!

YOUNG ODYSSEUS: Hermes! I'd love to chat, but Circe turned my crew into pigs and I must save them.

HERMES: Take this herb.

YOUNG ODYSSEUS: Okay. Thanks?

HERMES: Eat it.

YOUNG ODYSSEUS: All right. Pushy-pushy. Mmmm, tasty.

HERMES: The herb will stop the pig spell from working.

YOUNG ODYSSEUS: Ahhh! Good!

HERMES: Also, after she falls in love with you, ask her to change your crew back.

PENELOPE: Excuse me. After she what?! *(she's ignored)*

YOUNG ODYSSEUS: Sure. Can I go now?

PENELOPE: Hello?! *(stomps foot, still ignored; upset off to side)*

HERMES: Fine. YOU'RE WELCOME, by the way. *(to audience)* No one appreciates the messenger. Humph. *(exits)*

YOUNG ODYSSEUS: *(yells)* Circe! I've come to save my crew!

CIRCE: *(enters with cookie)* Odysseus! Perfect timing! Cookie?

YOUNG ODYSSEUS: I love cookies! *(eats)*

CIRCE: Wait, why aren't you a pig?

YOUNG ODYSSEUS: Because I've got a magic herb to protect me!

CIRCE: Drat. You know, you're kind of cute.

PENELOPE: That's it!! *(approaches CIRCE)*

YOUNG ODYSSEUS: *(holds PENELOPE back)* Let ME handle this. *(draws sword)* Un-pig my crew!

CIRCE: Anything for you... darling. *(snaps fingers and CREW enters no longer pigs)*

CREW 3: Oh man, I think I ate garbage.

CREW 2: Oh! I've got another one! What's a pig's favorite play? HAMlet! *(CREW groans)* No, HAMalot. *(CREW groans louder)* Dear Evan HAMson? *(CREW really annoyed)*. HAMilton!!!

CREW 4: *(to CREW 2)* No. PLEASE, make it stop.

CREW 1: *(to audience)* We stayed with Circe for a year...

PENELOPE: WHAT!?!?!

ODYSSEUS: *(shrugs)* She made really good cookies!

CREW 2: Odysseus, it is time you began to think about going home.

YOUNG ODYSSEUS: Yeah, you're probably right. Circe, thanks for the hospitality, but we should be going.

CIRCE: Fine. You can leave.

PENELOPE: About time. *(CIRCE and PENELOPE glare at each other)*

CIRCE: But first, you must go to Hades to consult the blind prophet Teiresias.

TELEMACHUS: You're going to the underworld? Yes!

YOUNG ODYSSEUS: Do we have to? Prophets are soooo depressing.

CIRCE: Yes. Teiresias will tell you what you must do to get home.

YOUNG ODYSSEUS: *(sigh)* Okay. Crew, we're off to Hades!

CREW: AWWWWW!

CIRCE: Bye, bye, little piggies! *(oinks)*

(ALL but YOUNG ODYSSES exit)

ACT 1 SCENE 4

Sirens and Scylla

(YOUNG ODYSSEUS enters)

YOUNG ODYSSEUS: *(to audience)* So, I just returned from the underworld. We have quite the adventures ahead. Unfortunatly, all my crew doesn't make it... actually, none of them do.

(CREW enters)

CREW 1: How was the meeting with Hade's prophet?

YOUNG ODYSSEUS: Ummm... excellent. I'm going to make it home!

CREW 2: And us?

YOUNG ODYSSEUS: Oh, look! Danger! *(points offstage)*

CREW 3: We soon came upon the first of many dangers.

YOUNG ODYSSEUS: Okay, here come the Sirens. Take this wax and stuff it in your ears. Now, tie me up!

CREW 4: What?

YOUNG ODYSSEUS: TIE ME UP! You won't hear the Siren's song because of the wax. But I want to be the first to hear it and live. Apparently, it's a catchy tune!

(CREW ties him up, starts speaking loudly)

CREW 1: You know, I'm not so sure this job was worth it.

CREW 2: I know, cannibals, pigs, monsters, now this!

CREW 3: Yeah, Odysseus is strange.

YOUNG ODYSSEUS: I heard that!

CREW 4: Oh, sorry!

(CREW starts rowing; SIRENS enter, say lines sing-song)

SIREN 1: Oh, brave Odysseus.

SIREN 2: Hero of men.

SIREN 1: Come to us...

SIREN 2: And never leave again! *(ALL laugh evilly)*

YOUNG ODYSSEUS: Okay, you can untie me now.

(CREW looks confused, can't hear him; YOUNG ODYSSEUS mimes untying)

CREW 2: Oh, sure thing, captain!

CREW 1: NO! He'll take us straight to the Sirens and they will eat us all!

YOUNG ODYSSEUS: They can't possibly eat ALL of us. I'm sure I'LL be okay!

CREW 2: Sorry, boss!

SIREN 1: Come closer to us...

SIREN 2: Your future will reveal...

SIREN 1: Secrets no man knows...

SIREN 2: *(to SIREN 1)* Odysseus will make a nice meal!

YOUNG ODYSSEUS: Untie me or else!!!

CREW 3: The captain looks mad!

CREW 4: Row faster!

SIRENS: *(SIRENS turn angry and reach for the ship)* NOOO! You mustn't escape!

CREW 1: This isn't the first time that we have been in danger! ROW!

(CREW rows furiously)

SIRENS: NOOOOOOOOOOOOOOOOOOOO!!! *(exit melodramatically)*

YOUNG ODYSSEUS: *(to the audience)* We sailed out of earshot and the crew untied me.

CREW 4: Whew. Glad that's over.

ODYSSEUS: *(enters, to audience)* Then Scylla, a 6-headed monster, pounced down and snatched up four of my crew.

(arms reach through the curtains and snatch CREW backstage)

CREW 1: WHAT IS HAPPENING?!?

(screaming backstage)

CREW 4: *(enters to YOUNG ODYSSEUS)* Did you know that was going to happen?

YOUNG ODYSSEUS: Uh... no? Keep rowing! We're almost past her.

CREW 2: *(enters)* That was terrible.

CREW 3: *(enters)* Yeah, that's the third time I've died in this show!

(CREW rows)

ACT 1 SCENE 6
Forbidden Cows

CREW 2: Look! Land!

YOUNG ODYSSEUS: Oh! I almost forgot; we can't stop here!

CREW: WHAT?!

YOUNG ODYSSEUS: It is the most dangerous place yet. Keep going!

CREW 1: They're just a bunch of cows, boss.

CREW 3: Maybe they are mutant cows that will eat us.

CREW 4: I'm tired of being eaten. I need to rest.

CREW 2: Me too!

CREW 1: I'm just tired!

CREW 3: Come on, sir. Let us stop.

YOUNG ODYSSEUS: Alright. Alright. But, you MUST promise not to harm a single cow.

CREW: Promise!

ODYSSEUS: *(to audience)* We came ashore and fell fast asleep. But, during the night, Zeus raised a great gale of wind, causing a hurricane.

CREW 1: Looks like we are stuck here.

YOUNG ODYSSEUS: We have lots of food on the ship. Remember, do NOT kill any cows!

CREW: Yes, sir! No cows!

ODYSSEUS: The hurricane blew for an entire month...

ALL: A MONTH!?!?

ODYSSEUS: We ran out of food. The days were long. I left my crew to take a nap. *(YOUNG ODYSSEUS exits)*

CREW 2: He naps at the strangest times.

CREW 3: I've never been this hungry in my life.

(COW enters)

COW: Moo.

CREW 4: Look! There's a nice, juicy hamburger. I-I-I mean cow.

COW: Moo?

CREW 1: Let's get it!

COW: Moo!!!

(CREW chases COW offstage, moo sounds from backstage, CREW enters licking their lips carrying "hamburger" supplies)

CREW 4: Now that hit the spot.

YOUNG ODYSSEUS: *(enters; sees hamburger paraphernalia)* Come on! I told you ONE thing. DO NOT eat the cows!

CREW 3: Sorry, boss. But it was only one.

CREW 4: And it was DELICIOUS!

CREW 1: Finally, the wind died down, and we set sail with full bellies!

(CREW rows)

CREW 2: As soon as we were away from the island, a black cloud formed over our ship.

CREW 3: It's Zeus!!!

ZEUS: *(enters)* Helios says you ate Bessie! My favorite bovine! *(stirs up a storm, ALL blow around stage)*

YOUNG ODYSSEUS: Told you not to eat the cows!

ODYSSEUS: *(to audience)* Zeus let fly his thunderbolts, the ship caught on fire, and the crew fell into the sea.

CREW 3: I guess this is it for us.

CREW 1: Nice knowing you!

CREW 4: That burger was worth it!!!

(CREW exits screaming, ZEUS exits happy)

ACT 2 SCENE 1

The Gods Interfere

(PENELOPE enters)

PENELOPE: Are you STILL telling this story?

ODYSSEUS: Hey, it was 20 years! *(to audience)* So, I floated to the Island of Calypso.

PENELOPE: She was nice and helped you?

ODYSSEUS: She captured me and held me in a cave.

CALYPSO: *(enters)* What? Can't a girl keep a guy in a cave until he agrees to marry her?!

PENELOPE: *(to CALYPSO)* I didn't have to capture him to get him to marry ME.

CALYPSO: *(shrugs)* Whatever. *(to YOUNG ODYSSEUS)* Let's go... prisoner.

(CALYPSO and YOUNG ODYSSEUS exit opposite PENELOPE and ODYSSEUS)

HERMES: *(enters)* But, as the years went by, the gods decided it was time for Odysseus to go home. I met with Zeus to discuss.

(enter ZEUS)

ZEUS: Hermes, Odysseus been there seven years. Poseidon won't kill Odysseus. Instead, he torments him by preventing him from getting home. Avenging his son.

HERMES: Well, his son wasn't being a very good host, eating his guests and all.

ZEUS: True. Go to tell Calypso to let Odysseus go.

HERMES: Who, me?

ZEUS: You ARE the god of messages.

HERMES: Can't I just text her? Maybe a video call?

ZEUS: NO! Now get going! Shoo!

(ZEUS exits as HERMES walks around stage mocking Zeus)

ACT 2 SCENE 2
Calypso

HERMES: Hello? Calypso?

CALYPSO: *(enters)* Oh, hello Hermes. What are YOU doing here?

HERMES: Nice place ya got here. Zeus sent me.

CALYPSO: Okaaaaay.

HERMES: Zeus says you must let Odysseus go.

CALYPSO: Really? *(full of rage)* Aghhhh! You gods ought to be ashamed of yourselves! You're just mad a goddess is in love with a mortal man!

HERMES: Hey, don't kill the messenger! Literally. Don't. Well, you can't anyway. Gods are immortal! Ha, ha!

CALYPSO: ARGH!

HERMES: Anyway, you know what happens if you say no to the big guy.

(HERMES makes a slit throat motion)

CALYPSO: FINE! I'll send him away.

HERMES: Great! I'm out of here! *(exits)*

CALYPSO: *(calls offstage)* Odysseus! Come here, darling!

ODYSSEUS: *(enters, sad)* What now?

CALYPSO: I'm sending you away. You can make yourself a raft. Don't be too sad, darling. Zeus insists it be so.

ODYSSEUS: YIPPEE!

CALYPSO: DON'T BE TOO SAD, DARLING!

ODYSSEUS: Oh, I mean, bummer. But a raft? I don't know if that's a good idea. You know, Poseidon.

CALYPSO: Well, if you want to stay...

ODYSSEUS: No! No, no. Raft is good!

CALYPSO: Oh well. Easy come, easy go. *(exits)*

ODYSSEUS: Off I sailed, until, of course, Poseidon noticed me.

POSEIDON: *(enters)* Who's that there? Is that Odysseus? He thinks he can just float home after blinding MY son!

ODYSSEUS: Poseidon gathered his clouds together, grasped his trident, stirred it around the sea, and roused the rage of every wind that blows.

POSEIDON: Oh yeah, I did! Winds from every direction hit Odysseus and his silly little raft all at once!

(POSEIDON making magical gestures while ODYSSEUS mimes thrashing in ocean)

ODYSSEUS: I was thrown from the raft into the crashing waves.

POSEIDON: Ha! Take that!

ODYSSEUS: But I was able to swim back and climb on.

POSEIDON: REALLY?!?

ODYSSEUS: Poseidon sent a terrible great wave and destroyed my raft.

POSEIDON: Take that!

ODYSSEUS: Then, I got on a plank of wood.

POSEIDON: This guy never dies! I give up. *(exits)*

ODYSSEUS: I floated until I made it to shore. Long story short...

TELEMACHUS: *(sticks head out)* Too late.

ACT 2 SCENE 3

Odysseus Returns

ODYSSEUS: I finally made it home! I went to my house as a beggar. *(changes outfit)*

(PENELOPE, TELEMACHUS, ANTINOUS, and SUITORS enter)

PENELOPE: *(to the suitors)* Listen up, boys. I have a great idea! This is the bow of Odysseus. Whomsoever of you shall string, and send his arrow through each one of twelve axes, I will marry.

(SUITORS cheer)

SUITOR 1: *(trying to string bow and failing miserably)* Ugh. This is too hard. Next! *(passes bow to SUITOR 2)*

SUITOR 2: I think I can. I think I can... *(struggles)*

ANTINOUS: Give me that! *(struggles)* This bow is impossible. Let's just forget this ever happened.

(SUITORS all agree)

ODYSSEUS: I'd like to try it.

ANTINOUS: You?!? Keep quiet without getting into a quarrel with men younger than yourself.

(SUITORS cheer in agreement)

PENELOPE: ENOUGH! Are you afraid he will make you all look like fools?

TELEMACHUS: Don't upset yourself, mother. Why don't we go get some water backstage? I don't think we need to see this next scene.

PENELOPE: Okay, son, if you think that's best.

(PENELOPE and TELEMACHUS exit; ODYSSEUS takes the bow and strings it, then shoots an arrow off-stage; SUITORS are awestruck)

ACT 2 Scene 4

The Suitors' Demise

ODYSSEUS: Dogs, did you think that I should not come back? You ate my food, mistreated my servants, and wooed my wife. You have feared neither God nor man, and now you shall die.

SUITOR 1: It's Odysseus!

SUITOR 2: Oh no. Scatter!

(SUITORS run around screaming)

ODYSSEUS: Antinous!

ANTINOUS: Who me?

(ODYSSEUS kills ANTINOUS; SUITORS see ANTINOUS, then scream)

SUITOR 1: Have mercy!

SUITOR 2: Yes! What he said!

ODYSSEUS: Let me think about it. Nope. *(to audience)* Since this part is a bit gruesome, we will skip it. But to summarize, they all died. *(snaps fingers, suitors fall dead)*

PENELOPE: *(enters with TELEMACHUS)* Hello stranger. A mighty big pile of bodies you've got there.

TELEMACHUS: This is TOTALLY a Greek play. Now THAT'S an ending! *(bows)*

ODYSSEUS: Exactly. An epic story must have an EPIC ending. And THIS is the original epic story.

TELEMACHUS: Does epic mean, like, super long?

ODYSSEUS: Yes. Wife, it is me, Odysseus! *(sheds costume)*

PENELOPE: *(running towards ODYSSEUS in slow motion)* O-dyss-e-us!

ODYSSEUS: Pe-nel-o-pe! *(running towards PENELOPE in slow motion)*

TELEMACHUS: Gag-me!

PENELOPE: And we all lived happily ever after.

ANTINOUS: Um, excuse me?

SUITOR 1: Does this look happy?

SUITOR 2: We just got slaughtered, remember?

ODYSSEUS: Ugh, that was several lines ago.

TELEMACHUS: Yeah, get over it already.

(SUITORS die again)

PENELOPE: As I said, HAPPILY EVER AFTER!

THE END

PlayingWithPlays.com

NOTES

The 25-Minute or so
THE ODYSSEY
for Kids
by Homer
Creatively modified by
Amanda Ruby & Brendan P. Kelso
20-32+ Actors

CAST OF CHARACTERS:

ODYSSEUS: our hero, on a long work trip

YOUNG ODYSSEUS: our hero, but younger

PENELOPE: his smart wife

TELEMACHUS: their son

CREW 1: member of Odysseus's crew

CREW 2: member of Odysseus's crew

CREW 3: member of Odysseus's crew

CREW 4: member of Odysseus's crew

CREW 5: member of Odysseus's crew

CREW 6: member of Odysseus's crew

[1]**CYCLOPS:** a hideous beast with one eye (for now)

[2]**TOWNSPERSON 1:** someone who lives in town

[5]**TOWNSPERSON 2:** someone else who lives in town

[3]**OGRE 1:** likes to eat people

[4]**OGRE 2:** likes to smash things

[7]**CIRCE:** a lady who loves animals

[6]**HERMES:** mischievous Greek god and messenger

[8]**TEIRESIAS:** a dead prophet

[6]**SIREN 1:** a deadly singer

[7]**SIREN 2:** another deadly singer
[9]**SIREN 3:** alas, yet another
[10]**SIREN 4:** and yes... a fourth!
[5]**ATHENA:** Greek goddess of wisdom
[4]**ZEUS:** Greek god of the sky - the big guy
[8]**CALYPSO:** wants to marry Odysseus
[3]**POSEIDON:** Greek god of the sea
[6]**SUITOR 1:** wants to marry Penelope
[7]**SUITOR 2:** wants to marry Penelope
[9]**SUITOR 3:** also, wants to marry Penelope
[10]**SUITOR 4:** and yes, Penelope
[2]**ANTINOUS:** the worst suitor (also, wants Penelope)
[1]**COW:** it's a cow, or lunch, depends on your perspective
SCYLLA: Nonspeaking, 6 headed monster - offstage
Extras can play townspeople, crew members, suitors, sirens all these parts have no lines, but you can add some if you like!

The same actors can play the following parts:

[1]**CYCLOPES and COW**
[2]**TOWNSPERSON and ANTINOUS**
[3]**OGRE and POSEIDON**
[4]**OGRE and ZEUS**
[5]**TOWNSPERSON and ATHENA**
[6]**HERMES, SIREN, and SUITOR**
[7]**CIRCE, SIREN, and SUITOR**
[8]**TEIRESIAS and CALYPSO**
[9]**SIREN and SUITOR**
[10]**SIREN and SUITOR**

ACT 1 SCENE 1
Odysseus is Home

(PENELOPE and ODYSSEUS run toward each other, TELEMACHUS follows)

ODYSSEUS: Penelope! I'm home!

PENELOPE: Finally! Odysseus, this is your son, Telemachus.

ODYSSEUS: *(baby talk)* Daddy missed you!

TELEMACHUS: Ahh, yeah, you've been gone, like, 20 years. Not quite a baby anymore.

ODYSSEUS: Oh, right... dude! *(awkward high-five; TELEMACHUS rolls eyes)*

PENELOPE: *(to audience)* And we all lived happily ever after. *(ODYSSEUS and PENELOPE bow)*

TELEMACHUS: Wait, what? We literally just started. These people came to see a play. *(to audience)* Right? *(gets audience to cheer)*

ALL: *(everyone thinks)* Hmmm.

PENELOPE: Well... Odysseus, you could tell us what you've been doing these past TWO DECADES.

ODYSSEUS: Ummm... nothing?

PENELOPE: Hmmm, nice try. Cough it up.

ODYSSEUS: Well, okay.

(YOUNG ODYSSEUS and CREW enter rowing)

ACT 1 SCENE 2

The Cyclops

ODYSSEUS: *(to audience)* Once upon a time, on the way home from the great Trojan War, a hurricane pushed us off course. *(ODYSSEUS sees YOUNG ODYSSEUS)* Aww, look how young I looked!

(YOUNG ODYSSEUS clears throat)

ODYSSEUS: Sorry, go ahead.

CREW 1: We've been rowing for months!

CREW 2: Look! Land!

CREW 3: It's full of flowers!

CREW 4: And the people look SOOOO happy!

YOUNG ODYSSEUS: NO. No, no, no, no! My buddy Jack has been there for decades, just eating flowers and staring at a wall. We are NOT stopping there!

CREW: Awwww. *(continue rowing)*

ODYSSEUS: We sailed until we came to the land of the Cyclops. *(enter CYCLOPS)* He was a horrid creature, not like a human being at all!

CYCLOPS: I resent that.

ODYSSEUS: No. RESEMBLE is the word you're looking for. *(CYCLOPS glares)* He stuck us in a cave, grabbed two of my crew, and ate them. *(CYCLOPS eats CREW 1 and 2, they die)*

CREW 1 & 2: Hey!

PENELOPE: He. Ate. Them? *(retches)*

ODYSSEUS: Yeah.

CYCLOPS: In my defense, I was hungry.

ODYSSEUS: Then he ate two more! *(eats 3 and 4, they die)* And yep, another two!

CREW 5: Ahhh, man.

CREW 6: And I thought swabbing the deck would be the worst part.

(CYCLOPS eats 5 and 6, they die)

CYCLOPS: *(burps)* Sorry. Continue.

YOUNG ODYSSEUS: You ought to be ashamed of yourself.

CYCLOPS: I know, but I don't get many visitors.

YOUNG ODYSSEUS: That's because you eat them!

CYCLOPS: That's true. What's your name?

YOUNG ODYSSEUS: My name is Noman. Please, drink this juice.

CYCLOPS: Don't mind if I do. Cheers. *(drinks)* That is good. More, please!

ODYSSEUS: And I gave him more. Lots more!

CYCLOPS: *(to audience)* I will eat all of Noman's crew! But I will save Noman for last. He looks tasty! *(yawns)* Wow, this juice makes me sleepy.

ODYSSEUS: As he spoke, he fell to the ground. I blinded him!

CYCLOPS: Do you have to?

YOUNG ODYSSEUS: Yeah, I do.

CYCLOPS: Well, if you must.

YOUNG ODYSSEUS: I must. *(blinds CYCLOPES)*

CYCLOPS: Ahhhh! My eye!!! *(stumbles around)*

ODYSSEUS: Cyclops made such a ruckus the townspeople came.

TOWNSPERSON 1: *(enters)* What's going on? Surely no man is trying to kill YOU!

CYCLOPS: *("no-man")* Noman is killing me! Noman is killing me!

TOWNSPERSON 2: Well, if no man is killing you, keep it down. People are trying to sleep! *(exits)*

ODYSSEUS: Then we escaped.

TELEMACHUS: You are crafty.

ODYSSEUS: Yes. Yes, I am.

CYCLOPS: I'll get you! *(tries to grab YOUNG ODYSSEUS)*

YOUNG ODYSSEUS: *(dodges CYCLOPS)* Neener, neener, boo, boo! *(sticks tongue at CYCLOPS)*

PENELOPE: Now, you're being just mean.

ODYSSEUS: Really? He ate six of my crew. Six!

CREW: Yeah!

PENELOPE: Fine.

YOUNG ODYSSEUS: *(to CYCLOPS)* Also, my real name is Odysseus! Ha, ha!!!

CYCLOPS: I'm telling my dad! *(exits)*

ODYSSEUS: Unfortunately, his dad was Poseidon, God of the sea.

TELEMACHUS: His dad was Poseidon?! Dude, you are so ruined!

ODYSSEUS & YOUNG ODYSSEUS: Right?!

(ALL exit)

ACT 1 SCENE 3

Circe

(PENELOPE, TELEMACHAUS, and CREW enter)

CREW 6: We arrived at the Aeolian Island.

PENELOPE: Wait a minute. Who are you? Didn't you just get eaten?

CREW 6: Who, me? No. Maybe... I have no idea what you're talking about.

PENELOPE: *(suspicious)* Okay... go on.

CREW 4: Before we left, the Aeolian king gave Odysseus a bag of wind.

PENELOPE: A bag of what?

CREW 5: Wind! See! *(holds up bag)* It holds the bad winds so we could sail home safely.

CREW 6: Can I hold it?!

CREW 5: Sure! *(CREW 6 runs around the stage playing with it)*

PENELOPE: Well, that's good!

CREW 2: It was, until Odysseus took a nap.

TELEMACHUS: What happened?

CREW 4: Some curious crew member, NOT ME, *(ALL CREW look sternly at CREW 6)* opened the bag and the wind flew howling forth and raised a storm that carried us back out to sea.

(CREW 6 opens bag and ALL get blown around stage)

YOUNG ODYSSEUS: *(enters stretching)* What is happening here? *(ALL stop)* Why aren't we on shore yet?

CREW 5: About that...

(ALL CREW point to CREW 6)

CREW 6: Sorry boss.

YOUNG ODYSSEUS: What?! You're first to be eaten next time!

CREW 6: Okay. Next time?

ODYSSEUS: *(enters)* So, we sailed on until we reached the city of the Laestrygonians.

(CREW rows)

PENELOPE: OK, and then?

ODYSSEUS: Then ogres! They're giants and cannibals.

TELEMACHUS: Wasn't the Cyclops a giant and a cannibal?

ODYSSEUS: Yes, but he had one eye and was the son of a god.

TELEMACHUS: Oh. Right. Totally different. Go on.

YOUNG ODYSSEUS: Okay, crew, let's stop here and rest.

CREW 2: Aye, aye, captain.

CREW 3: *(to audience)* Oh, look! Ogres!

(OGRES enter)

OGRE 1: Come on, this is our part!

OGRE 2: You eat. I'll crush.

(YOUNG ODYSSEUS refers to CREW 6)

YOUNG ODYSSEUS: Yo, you're up.

CREW 6: I get eaten again?! *(gets eaten)*

YOUNG ODYSSEUS: Told you!

CREW 3: Oh, goody! This time I get crushed by a boulder, instead of eaten! *(gets crushed)*

OGRE 1: Nice work!

OGRE 2: I love my job. I'm going to throw boulders at their ships and sink them.

OGRE 1: OK, have fun! I'm going to take a nap. Eating humans makes me sleepy.

(OGRES exit, CREW rises, rowing)

CREW 4: *(to audience)* We escaped to our one hidden ship and sailed on until we came to the island where Circe lives.

YOUNG ODYSSEUS: Look up ahead. I see a house!

CREW 1: I think I'll just stay here on the ship.

CREW 3: Oh, come on, you big baby!

YOUNG ODYSSEUS: Yeah, don't be a baby. You go and I'LL stay with the ship. *(stands to side)*

CREW 1: Aw, man!

(CREW walks around stage)

CIRCE: *(enters singing)* Why, hello strangers! Come on in! I'll get you some cookies!

CREW 3: Yes! Cookies!!!

(CREW chants "cookies, cookies, cookies...")

CREW 1: *(to audience)* But the food was enchanted, and we turned into pigs.

TELEMACHUS: Pigs? Really?

CREW 1: Yes, really. Oink!

(CREW starts acting like pigs)

CIRCE: Here you go, little piggies! *(tosses treats to pigs)*

CREW 1: This is HOGwash!

CREW 2: Yeah, what is this place, HOGwarts?

CREW 3: Oh, are we doing jokes? What's my pig name? *(CREW shrugs)* Chris P. Bacon!

CREW 1: Ugh. Enough. This is humiliating. Oink.

CIRCE: Come on little piggies. We're off to market!

(CIRCE and CREW exit)

ODYSSEUS: The god Hermes saw what happened and decided to help. After, he laughed at us.

(HERMES enters; laughing)

HERMES: God of deliveries here!

YOUNG ODYSSEUS: Hermes! I'd love to chat, but Circe turned my crew into pigs and I must save them.

HERMES: Take this herb.

YOUNG ODYSSEUS: Okay. Thanks?

HERMES: Eat it.

YOUNG ODYSSEUS: All right. Pushy-pushy. Mmmm, tasty.

HERMES: The herb will stop the pig spell from working.

YOUNG ODYSSEUS: Ahhh! Good!

HERMES: Also, after she falls in love with you, ask her to change your crew back.

PENELOPE: Excuse me. After she what?! *(she's ignored)*

YOUNG ODYSSEUS: Sure. Can I go now?

PENELOPE: Hello?! *(stomps foot, still ignored; upset off to side)*

HERMES: Fine. YOU'RE WELCOME, by the way. *(to audience)* No one appreciates the messenger. Humph. *(exits)*

YOUNG ODYSSEUS: *(yells)* Circe! I've come to save my crew!

CIRCE: *(enters with cookie)* Odysseus! Perfect timing! Cookie?

YOUNG ODYSSEUS: I love cookies! *(eats)*

CIRCE: Wait, why aren't you a pig?

YOUNG ODYSSEUS: Because I've got a magic herb to protect me!

CIRCE: Drat. You know, you're kind of cute.

PENELOPE: That's it!! *(approaches CIRCE)*

YOUNG ODYSSEUS: *(holds PENELOPE back)* Let ME handle this. *(draws sword)* Un-pig my crew!

CIRCE: Anything for you... darling. *(snaps fingers and CREW enters no longer pigs)*

CREW 2: Oh man, I think I ate garbage.

CREW 3: Oh! I've got another one! What's a pig's favorite play? HAMlet! *(CREW groans)* No, HAMalot. *(CREW groans louder)* Dear Evan HAMson? *(CREW really annoyed)*. HAMilton!!!

CREW 4: *(to CREW 3)* No. PLEASE, make it stop.

CREW 6: *(to audience)* We stayed with Circe for a year...

PENELOPE: WHAT!?!?!

ODYSSEUS: *(shrugs)* She made really good cookies!

CREW 5: Odysseus, it is time you began to think about going home.

YOUNG ODYSSEUS: Yeah, you're probably right. Circe, thanks for the hospitality, but we should be going.

CIRCE: Fine. You can leave.

PENELOPE: About time. *(CIRCE and PENELOPE glare at each other)*

CIRCE: But first, you must go to Hades to consult the blind prophet Teiresias.

TELEMACHUS: You're going to the underworld? Yes!

YOUNG ODYSSEUS: Do we have to? Prophets are soooo depressing.

CIRCE: Yes. Teiresias will tell you what you must do to get home.

YOUNG ODYSSEUS: *(sigh)* Okay. Crew, we're off to Hades!

CREW: AWWWWW!

CIRCE: Bye, bye, little piggies! *(oinks)*

(ALL but YOUNG ODYSSES exit)

ACT 1 SCENE 4

Hades

YOUNG ODYSSEUS: *(to audience)* When we reached Hades, Teiresias appeared.

TEIRESIAS: *(enters)* Odysseus, why have you left the light of day and come down to visit the dead?

YOUNG ODYSSEUS: Wow, you can see pretty well for being blind.

TEIRESIAS: What can I say? It's a gift.

YOUNG ODYSSEUS: Circe said you would help me get home.

TEIRESIAS: Well, Poseidon won't make it an easy journey.

YOUNG ODYSSEUS: Tell me something I don't know.

TEIRESIAS: First you will come to the Sirens who enchant all who come near them. Make sure your crew can't hear the Siren's song. You can listen, but no one has EVER heard it and survived.

YOUNG ODYSSEUS: Really? Challenge accepted. What else?

TEIRESIAS: Once you pass the Sirens, there are two ways you can go. In one direction, you will pass Scylla's cave.

YOUNG ODYSSEUS: Is she nice?

TEIRESIAS: She is a monster with six heads. She will eat some of your crew.

YOUNG ODYSSEUS: What is it with monsters constantly eating my crew?!

TEIRESIAS: Don't know. Maybe they taste like chicken?

YOUNG ODYSSEUS: Ugh. So, we will go the other way.

TEIRESIAS: The other way has the sucking whirlpool of Charybdis. Only Jason and his Argonauts have sailed and got through.

YOUNG ODYSSEUS: Then I can do it, too.

TEIRESIAS: He was helped by a god. Better stick to the Scylla side.

YOUNG ODYSSEUS: Are you sure?

TEIRESIAS: One word. Poseidon. Better to lose some crew than your whole crew... yet.

YOUNG ODYSSEUS: Yeah, ok. Wait, yet?

TEIRESIAS: Helios, the sun god, has an island full of cows. DO. NOT. EAT. THEM. Think of nothing but getting home. Otherwise, your ship and crew will be destroyed.

YOUNG ODYSSEUS: Isn't there an easier way to get home?

TEIRESIAS: No.

YOUNG ODYSSEUS: Alrighty then.

TEIRESIAS: YOU will make it home, after much suffering, but all of your crew will die.

YOUNG ODYSSEUS: ALL of my crew?

TEIRESIAS: When you return, your house will be overrun with suitors trying to marry your wife. You will take revenge upon them.

YOUNG ODYSSEUS: Okay. Sounds like fun. But I survive, right?

TEIRESIAS: You shall live a long life and death shall come to you from the sea, but you will be at peace.

YOUNG ODYSSEUS: Well, thanks for your depressing prophecy.

TEIRESIAS: They usually are. You might not want to tell your crew about the whole dying thing. I foresee that being a problem.

YOUNG ODYSSEUS: Yeah. Good idea.

TEIRESIAS: Bye, bye! *(exits)*

ACT 1 SCENE 5

Sirens and Scylla

(CREW enters)

CREW 1: How was the meeting?

YOUNG ODYSSEUS: Ummm... excellent. I'm going to make it home!

CREW 2: And us?

YOUNG ODYSSEUS: Oh, look! Danger! *(points offstage)*

CREW 5: We soon came upon the first of many dangers.

YOUNG ODYSSEUS: Okay, here come the Sirens. Take this wax and stuff it in your ears. Now, tie me up!

CREW 6: What?

YOUNG ODYSSEUS: TIE ME UP! You won't hear the Siren's song because of the wax. But I want to be the first to hear it and live. Apparently, it's a catchy tune!

(CREW ties him up, starts speaking loudly)

CREW 4: You know, I'm not so sure this job was worth it.

CREW 5: I know, cannibals, pigs, monsters, now this!

CREW 6: Yeah, Odysseus is strange.

YOUNG ODYSSEUS: I heard that!

CREW 6: Oh, sorry!

(CREW starts rowing; SIRENS enter, say lines sing-song)

SIREN 1: Oh, brave Odysseus.

SIREN 2: Hero of men.

SIREN 3: Come to us...

SIREN 4: And never leave again! *(ALL laugh evilly)*

YOUNG ODYSSEUS: Okay, you can untie me now.

(CREW looks confused, can't hear him; YOUNG ODYSSEUS mimes untying)

CREW 2: Oh, sure thing, captain!

CREW 1: NO! He'll take us straight to the Sirens and they will eat us all!

YOUNG ODYSSEUS: They can't possibly eat ALL of us. I'm sure I'LL be okay!

CREW 2: Sorry, boss!

SIREN 1: Come closer to us...

SIREN 2: Your future will reveal...

SIREN 3: Secrets no man knows...

SIREN 4: *(to SIREN 1)* Odysseus will make a nice meal!

YOUNG ODYSSEUS: Untie me or else!!!

CREW 5: The captain looks mad!

CREW 6: Row faster!

SIRENS: *(SIRENS turn angry and reach for the ship)* NOOO! You mustn't escape!

CREW 1: This isn't the first time that we have been in danger! ROW!

(CREW rows furiously)

SIRENS: NOOOOOOOOOOOOOOOOOOOOO!!! *(exit melodramatically)*

YOUNG ODYSSEUS: *(to the audience)* We sailed out of earshot and the crew untied me.

CREW 4: Whew. Glad that's over.

ODYSSEUS: *(enters, to audience)* Then Scylla pounced down and snatched up six of my crew.

(arms reach through the curtains and snatch CREW backstage)

CREW 5: WHAT IS HAPPENING?!?

(screaming backstage)

CREW 4: *(enters to YOUNG ODYSSEUS)* Did you know that was going to happen?

YOUNG ODYSSEUS: Uh... no? Keep rowing! We're almost past her.

CREW 2: *(enters)* That was terrible.

CREW 3: *(enters)* Yeah, that's the third time I've died in this show!

(CREW rows)

ACT 1 SCENE 6
Forbidden Cows

CREW 5: Look! Land!

YOUNG ODYSSEUS: Oh! I almost forgot; we can't stop here!

CREW: WHAT?!

YOUNG ODYSSEUS: It is the most dangerous place yet. Keep going!

CREW 5: They're just a bunch of cows, boss.

CREW 3: Maybe they are mutant cows that will eat us.

CREW 4: I'm tired of being eaten. I need to rest.

CREW 2: Me too!

CREW 6: I'm just tired!

CREW 1: Come on, sir. Let us stop.

YOUNG ODYSSEUS: Alright. Alright. But, you MUST promise not to harm a single cow.

CREW: Promise!

ODYSSEUS: *(to audience)* We came ashore and fell fast asleep. But, during the night, Zeus raised a great gale of wind, causing a hurricane.

CREW 1: Looks like we are stuck here.

YOUNG ODYSSEUS: We have lots of food on the ship. Remember, do NOT kill any cows!

CREW: Yes, sir! No cows!

ODYSSEUS: The hurricane blew for an entire month...

ALL: A MONTH!?!?

ODYSSEUS: We ran out of food. The days were long. I left my crew to take a nap. *(YOUNG ODYSSEUS exits)*

CREW 2: He naps at the strangest times.

CREW 3: I've never been this hungry in my life.

(COW enters)

COW: Moo.

CREW 4: Look! There's a nice, juicy hamburger. I-I-I mean cow.

COW: Moo?

CREW 5: Let's get it!

COW: Moo!!!

(CREW chases COW offstage, moo sounds from backstage, CREW enters licking their lips carrying "hamburger" supplies)

CREW 4: Now that hit the spot.

YOUNG ODYSSEUS: *(enters; sees hamburger paraphernalia)* Come on! I told you ONE thing. DO NOT eat the cows!

CREW 5: Sorry, boss. But it was only one.

CREW 4: And it was DELICIOUS!

CREW 1: Finally, the wind died down, and we set sail with full bellies!

(CREW rows)

CREW 2: As soon as we were away from the island, a black cloud formed over our ship.

CREW 3: It's Zeus!!!

ZEUS: *(enters)* Helios says you ate Bessie! My favorite bovine! *(stirs up a storm, ALL blow around stage)*

YOUNG ODYSSEUS: Told you not to eat the cows!

ODYSSEUS: *(to audience)* Zeus let fly his thunderbolts, the ship caught on fire, and the crew fell into the sea.

CREW 3: I guess this is it for us.

CREW 5: Nice knowing you!

CREW 4: That burger was worth it!!!

(CREW exits screaming, ZEUS exits happy)

ACT 2 SCENE 1

The Gods Interfere

(PENELOPE enters)

PENELOPE: Are you STILL telling this story?

ODYSSEUS: Hey, it was 20 years! *(to audience)* So, I floated to the Island of Calypso.

PENELOPE: She was nice and helped you?

ODYSSEUS: She captured me and held me in a cave.

CALYPSO: *(enters)* What? Can't a girl keep a guy in a cave until he agrees to marry her?!

PENELOPE: *(to CALYPSO)* I didn't have to capture him to get him to marry ME.

CALYPSO: *(shrugs)* Whatever. *(to YOUNG ODYSSEUS)* Let's go... prisoner.

(CALYPSO and YOUNG ODYSSEUS exit opposite PENELOPE and ODYSSEUS)

HERMES: *(enters)* But, as the years went by, the gods decided it was time for Odysseus to go home. I met with Zeus and Athena to discuss.

(enter ZEUS and ATHENA)

ATHENA: Poor Odysseus. Calypso won't let him go home, but he never gives up hope of seeing his family.

ZEUS: Yes, Athena, he's been there seven years. Poseidon won't kill Odysseus. Instead, he torments him by preventing him from getting home. Avenging his son.

ATHENA: Well, his son wasn't being a very good host, eating his guests and all. We should send Hermes to tell Calypso to let Odysseus go.

HERMES: Who, me?

ATHENA: You ARE the god of messages. Tell her we have made up our minds and she must listen to us.

HERMES: Can't I just text her? Maybe a video call?

ZEUS: NO! Now get going! Shoo!

(ZEUS and ATHENA exit as HERMES walks around stage mocking Zeus)

ACT 2 SCENE 2

Calypso

HERMES: Hello? Calypso?

CALYPSO: *(enters)* Oh, hello Hermes. What are YOU doing here?

HERMES: Nice place ya got here. Zeus sent me.

CALYPSO: Okaaaaay.

HERMES: Zeus says you must let Odysseus go.

CALYPSO: Really? *(full of rage)* Aghhhh! You gods ought to be ashamed of yourselves! You're just mad a goddess is in love with a mortal man!

HERMES: Hey, don't kill the messenger! Literally. Don't. Well, you can't anyway. Gods are immortal! Ha, ha!

CALYPSO: ARGH!

HERMES: Anyway, you know what happens if you say no to the big guy.

(HERMES makes a slit throat motion)

CALYPSO: FINE! I'll send him away.

HERMES: Great! I'm out of here! *(exits)*

CALYPSO: *(calls offstage)* Odysseus! Come here, darling!

ODYSSEUS: *(enters, sad)* What now?

CALYPSO: I'm sending you away. You can make yourself a raft. Don't be too sad, darling. Zeus insists it be so.

ODYSSEUS: YIPPEE!

CALYPSO: DON'T BE TOO SAD, DARLING!

ODYSSEUS: Oh, I mean, bummer. But a raft? I don't know if that's a good idea. You know, Poseidon.

CALYPSO: Well, if you want to stay...

ODYSSEUS: No! No, no. Raft is good!

CALYPSO: Oh well. Easy come, easy go. *(exits)*

ODYSSEUS: Off I sailed, until, of course, Poseidon noticed me.

POSEIDON: *(enters)* Who's that there? Is that Odysseus? He thinks he can just float home after blinding MY son!

ODYSSEUS: Poseidon gathered his clouds together, grasped his trident, stirred it around the sea, and roused the rage of every wind that blows.

POSEIDON: Oh yeah, I did! Winds from every direction hit Odysseus and his silly little raft all at once!

(POSEIDON making magical gestures while ODYSSEUS mimes thrashing in ocean)

ODYSSEUS: I was thrown from the raft into the crashing waves.

POSEIDON: Ha! Take that!

ODYSSEUS: But I was able to swim back and climb on.

POSEIDON: REALLY?!?

ODYSSEUS: Poseidon sent a terrible great wave and destroyed my raft.

POSEIDON: Take that!

ODYSSEUS: Then, I got on a plank of wood.

POSEIDON: This guy never dies! I give up. *(exits)*

ODYSSEUS: I floated until I made it to shore. Long story short...

TELEMACHUS: *(sticks head out)* Too late.

ACT 2 SCENE 3

Odysseus Returns

ATHENA: *(enters)* Hey buddy, it's me, Athena!

ODYSSEUS: Oh, hey.

ATHENA: I've been helping you this whole journey.

ODYSSEUS: You were HELPING me? Where were you when my crew were being eaten by various monsters?

ATHENA: In the dressing room. Don't be so dramatic. I knew YOU would survive. Now, I need to make you old and ugly, so no one can recognize you.

ODYSSEUS: Is that really necessary?

ATHENA: Yes. *(magic gesture; ODYSSEUS turns ugly)* Good luck! *(ATHENA exits)*

ODYSSEUS: I went to my house as a beggar.

(PENELOPE, TELEMACHUS, ANTINOUS, and SUITORS enter)

PENELOPE: *(to the suitors)* Listen up, boys. I have a great idea! This is the bow of Odysseus. Whomsoever of you shall string, and send his arrow through each one of twelve axes, I will marry.

(SUITORS cheer)

SUITOR 1: *(trying to string bow and failing miserably)* Ugh. This is too hard. Next! *(passes bow to SUITOR 2)*

SUITOR 2: I think I can. I think I can... *(struggles)*

ANTINOUS: Give me that! *(struggles)* This bow is impossible. Let's just forget this ever happened.

(SUITORS all agree)

ODYSSEUS: I'd like to try it.

ANTINOUS: You?!? Keep quiet without getting into a quarrel with men younger than yourself.

(SUITORS cheer in agreement)

PENELOPE: ENOUGH! Are you afraid he will make you all look like fools?

TELEMACHUS: Don't upset yourself, mother. Why don't we go get some water backstage? I don't think we need to see this next scene.

PENELOPE: Okay, son, if you think that's best.

(PENELOPE and TELEMACHUS exit; ODYSSEUS takes the bow and strings it, then shoots an arrow off-stage; SUITORS are awestruck)

ACT 2 Scene 4

The Suitors' Demise

ODYSSEUS: Dogs, did you think that I should not come back? You ate my food, mistreated my servants, and wooed my wife. You have feared neither God nor man, and now you shall die.

SUITOR 3: It's Odysseus!

SUITOR 4: Oh no. Scatter!

(SUITORS run around screaming)

ODYSSEUS: Antinous!

ANTINOUS: Who me?

(ODYSSEUS kills ANTINOUS; SUITORS see ANTINOUS, then scream)

SUITOR 2: Have mercy!

SUITOR 3: Yes! What he said!

ODYSSEUS: Let me think about it. Nope. *(to audience)* Since this part is a bit gruesome, we will skip it. But to summarize, they all died. *(snaps fingers, suitors fall dead)*

PENELOPE: *(enters with TELEMACHUS)* Hello stranger. A mighty big pile of bodies you've got there.

TELEMACHUS: This is TOTALLY a Greek play. Now THAT'S an ending! *(bows)*

ODYSSEUS: Exactly. An epic story must have an EPIC ending. And THIS is the original epic story.

TELEMACHUS: Does epic mean, like, super long?

ODYSSEUS: Yes. Wife, it is me, Odysseus! *(sheds costume)*

PENELOPE: *(running towards ODYSSEUS in slow motion)* O-dyss-e-us!

ODYSSEUS: Pe-nel-o-pe! *(running towards PENELOPE in slow motion)*

TELEMACHUS: Gag-me!

PENELOPE: And we all lived happily ever after.

ANTINOUS: Um, excuse me?

SUITOR 3: Does this look happy?

SUITOR 4: We just got slaughtered, remember?

ODYSSEUS: Ugh, that was several lines ago.

TELEMACHUS: Yeah, get over it already.

(SUITORS die again)

PENELOPE: As I said, HAPPILY EVER AFTER!

THE END

Pronunciation Key

ODYSSEUS: Oh-DI-see-uhs

TELEMACHUS: tul-LEH-muh-kuhs

TEIRESIAS: tee-REE-see-uhs

ANTINOUS: an-TI-now-uhs

CIRCE: SIR-see

LAESTRYGONIANS: less-try-go-nyans

AEILIAN: a-OH-lee-ahn

CHARYBDIS: kr-IB-duhs

SCYLLA: SKY-luh

Author's notes and Special Thanks

Special thanks to my theatre community for keeping me on my toes.
-Amanda

My biggest shout out goes to all the classrooms who workshopped my play! It is always so very awesome to have so many kids provide feedback! Even a couple got up an acted it out. One even did a set design from legos!

The classes who workshopped this play:

Ms. Shannon and Ms. Melanie's CC Challenge classes

Mr. Rod's Theatre 1 Classes Spring 2024

Magistra Laura AhMow and Magister Hood and his 9th grade class

David Ello's 23/24 6th Grade Drama students at Old Orchard Junior High. :-)

Special thanks always goes out to my Beta Readers: The Arnold Gals, Allison, Isidro, Christina, Melissa, Shauna, Darlene, Lisa M., Kayla, Bridget, Deanna, and Jamie!

Thank you all!

-Brendan P. Kelso
Break some legs!

Sneak Peeks at other
Playing With Plays books:

The Oresteia
for Kids

ATHENA: A conundrum! Too mighty is this matter. I know! We shall have a trial! I, of course, shall be judge, because, well, I AM the goddess of wisdom. And we will have a jury of Athenians. *(exits)*

CHORUS 8: Seriously, a trial? Boring!

CHORUS 9: Let's rip him to pieces.

CHORUS 7: I like how you think.

(CHORUS creeps toward ORESTES; ATHENA enters with JURY; CHORUS acts innocent, unfreezes ORESTES)

ATHENA: Let the trial begin. Jury, stand over there.

(EVERYONE takes their "court" positions; APOLLO enters)

CHORUS 8: Apollo, why are you here?

APOLLO: I came to defend Orestes.

CHORUS 9: You're not a lawyer!

APOLLO: I'm a god!

CHORUS 7: That does sound like a lawyer.

ATHENA: Hello, brother.

APOLLO: Yo! What up, Thena!

ATHENA: Alright! Let's begin. Tell the tale first and set the matter clear.

CHORUS 8: Orestes, hast then thy mother slain??

ORESTES: I slew her. I deny no word hereof.

CHORUS 9: We rest our case.

CHORUS 7: Off with his head!

ORESTES: Wait! I killed her, but Apollo told me to. Plus, she killed my father.

CHORUS 8: But, she was not kin by blood to him she slew.

CHORUS 9: Yeah, it's way worse to kill someone of your own blood.

CHORUS 7: Off with his head!

APOLLO: *(to ORESTES)* I got this, bro. *(to the JURY)* She was only his mom. The male is the parent! She was just a... a woman.

(EVERYONE gasps)

CHORUS 8: Hold me back! *(CHORUS 7 & 9 holds her back)*

ORESTES: *(to APOLLO)* Dude, I'm not sure that's the best defense.

APOLLO: Shhh... That he should die, a chieftain, and a king... by female hands! Shameful.

ATHENA: Ok, enough is said. Furies, do you rest your case?

CHORUS: Yes.

ATHENA: Apollo, do you rest your case?

APOLLO: *(looking at himself in a mirror)* What? Yeah, sure.

Christmas Carol
for Kids

(enter GHOST PRESENT wearing a robe and holding a turkey leg and a goblet)

GHOST PRESENT: Wake up, Scrooge! I am the Ghost of Christmas Present. Look upon me!

SCROOGE: I'm looking. Not that impressed. But let's get on with it.

GHOST PRESENT: Touch my robe! *(SCROOGE touches GHOST PRESENT's robe. Pause. They look at each other)* Er...it must be broken. Guess we walk. Come on. *(they begin walking downstage)*

SCROOGE: Where are we going?

GHOST PRESENT: Your employee, Bob Cratchit's house. Oh look, here we are.

(enter BOB, MRS. CRATCHIT, MARTHA CRATCHIT, and TINY TIM, who has a crutch in one hand; they are all holding bowls)

BOB: *(to audience)* Hi, we're the Cratchit family. We are a REALLY happy family!

MRS. CRATCHIT: *(to audience)* Yes, but we're REALLY poor, too. Thanks to HIS boss! *(pointing at BOB)*

MARTHA: *(to audience)* Yeah, as you can see our bowls are empty. *(shows empty bowl)* We practically survive off air.

TINY TIM: *(to audience)* But we're happy!

MRS. CRATCHIT: *(to audience; overly sappy)* Because we have each other.

TINY TIM: And love!

SCROOGE: *(to GHOST PRESENT)* Seriously, are they for real?

GHOST PRESENT: Yep! Adorable, isn't it?

BOB: A merry Christmas to us all.

TINY TIM: God bless us every one!

SCROOGE: Spirit, tell me if Tiny Tim will live.

GHOST PRESENT: *(puts hands to head as if looking into the future)* Ooooo, not so good....I see a vacant seat in the poor chimney corner, and a crutch without an owner. If SOMEBODY doesn't change SOMETHING, the child will die.

SCROOGE: No, no! Say he will be spared.

GHOST PRESENT: Nope, can't do that, sorry. Unless SOMEONE decides to change...hint, hint.

BOB: A Christmas toast to my boss, Mr. Scrooge! The founder of the feast!

MRS. CRATCHIT: *(angrily)* Oh sure, Mr. Scrooge! If he were here I'd give him a piece of my mind to feast upon. What an odious, stingy, hard, unfeeling man!

BOB: Dear, it's Christmas day. He's not THAT bad. *(Pause)* He's just... THAT sad. *(BOB holds up his bowl)* Come on, kids, to Scrooge! He probably needs it more than us!

MARTHA & TINY TIM: *(holding up their bowls)* To Scrooge!

MRS. CRATCHIT: *(muttering)* Thanks for nothing.

BOB: That's not nice.

MARTHA: And we Cratchits are ALWAYS nice. Read

the book, Mom.

MRS. CRATCHIT: Sorry.

(the CRATCHIT FAMILY exits)

SCROOGE: She called me odious! Do I really smell that bad?

GHOST PRESENT: Odious doesn't mean you stink. Although in this case you do... According to the dictionary, odious means "unequivocally detestable." I mean, you are a toad sometimes Mr. Scrooge.

SCROOGE: Wow... that's kind of ... mean.

Jekyll and Hyde
for Kids

UTTERSON: *(looks around)* Now, where is Hyde hiding?

NARRATOR: And they meet...

(enter HYDE)

UTTERSON: Mr. Hyde, I think?

HYDE: *(taken aback, and hisses)* That is my name. What's your issue?

UTTERSON: I am looking for Dr. Jekyll.

HYDE: He's not here.

UTTERSON: Let me see your face, sir.

HYDE: Why? Tell me how you know of me?

UTTERSON: We have common friends.

HYDE: *(snarls)* LIAR!!! *(suddenly exits)*

UTTERSON: Rude! *(to audience)* Did you see that murderous mixture of timidity and boldness? He seemed hardly human. I need to see Dr. Jekyll! *(walks across stage; knocks on door; POOLE enters)* Hello Poole, is Dr. Jekyll in?

POOLE: I'm sorry sir, but Dr. Jekyll is out.

UTTERSON: What can you tell me about Edward Hyde? I see he has a key to the back room.

POOLE: Ah, yes. Mr. Hyde has a key. We have orders to obey him.

UTTERSON: Thank you.

POOLE: Good day, sir. *(POOLE exits)*

UTTERSON: *(to audience)* That evil Hyde definitely has secrets of his own, black secrets. What has Jekyll gotten himself into?

(UTTERSON exits)

ACT 1 SCENE 3

Dr. Jekyll Was Quite at Ease

(enter DR. JEKYLL, UTTERSON)

NARRATOR: Soon, Dr. Jekyll hosted a party, and Utterson was determined to question his dear old friend...

JEKYLL: Thank you for coming to my pleasant dinner party. I always enjoy your company, Mr. Utterson.

UTTERSON: I've been wanting to speak to you, Jekyll. You know that will of yours?

JEKYLL: You are unfortunate in such a client. I never saw a man so distressed as you were by my will.

UTTERSON: You know I never approved of it.

JEKYLL: Yes, you have told me so.

UTTERSON: Well, I tell you again. Because I have learned more of young Hyde. What I heard was abominable.

JEKYLL: *(surprised)* Listen to me. DROP THIS. You do not understand my position.

UTTERSON: Jekyll, I am a man to be trusted. I am a lawyer. *(NARRATOR starts laughing; to NARRATOR)* Don't laugh.

NARRATOR: Sorry, you said "trust" and "lawyer" in the same sentence. And...yeah... My bad. Go on.

UTTERSON: *(to JEKYLL)* Tell me in confidence and I can get you out of it.

JEKYLL: I can be rid of Mr. Hyde when I choose. This is a private matter, and I beg of you to let it sleep.

UTTERSON: Fine, I will let it go... for now.

JEKYLL: Good.

The Legend of Sleepy Hollow for Kids

(enter DIEDRICH, stands behind podium)

DIEDRICH: This is a true story, based on fiction, which I heard secondhand from an old farmer, who doesn't exist. So it must be true or urban legend? Confused yet? Good! Hello! My name is Diedrich Knickerbocker, and I'm your narrator for today's creepy adventure. Our story takes place in 1790, in a sequestered glen, known by the name of SLEEPY HOLLOW. Speaking of creepy looking, check out this guy.

(enter ICHABOD whistling and reading a book titled: WITCHCRAFT)

ICHABOD: Oh, I do love these ghost stories!

DIEDRICH: Hey sir! Watch where you're going. There have been many terrors of the night down that path.

ICHABOD: Really?

DIEDRICH: Yes! There's a drowsy, dreamy influence that seems to hang over the land.

ICHABOD: Sounds fascinating!

DIEDRICH: No. Sounds spine-chilling! Why, in the name of all things weird, would you want to go THERE?!

ICHABOD: I am a student of supernatural stories and marvellous beliefs!

DIEDRICH: Well then, crazy's waiting for you just down the road!

ICHABOD: Oh goody! *(walks towards "town" offstage)*

DIEDRICH: I tried to warn him.

(ICHABOD enters, looks around)

ICHABOD: Well, this town looks like a wonderful place to stay for a while.

(enter WIVES who stop ICHABOD)

WIFE 1: And who might you be?

ICHABOD: My name, dear ladies, is Ichabod Crane. *(he bows)*

WIFE 2: And what do you do?

ICHABOD: I am a schoolmaster.

(WIVES look at each other happily)

WIFE 3: We are looking for a teacher.

ICHABOD: As well as a singing-master. *(starts singing)*

WIFE 4: That's fantastic!

ICHABOD: But, I'm afraid I don't have much money or a place to stay.

WIFE 1: That's ok. If you teach our children, we will gladly house and feed you... a total stranger!

WIFE 2: Yes. We don't believe in stranger danger here and you look smart, I think.

WIFE 3: That's right! We have a lot stranger things to worry about than random people coming through our town!

WIFE 4: Like marvellous tales of ghosts and goblins!

WIFE 1: And haunted fields!

WIFE 2: And haunted brooks!

WIFE 3: And haunted bridges!

WIFE 4: And haunted houses!

ICHABOD: And the supernatural?!

WIVES: Oh, yes!

ICHABOD: Then I'm staying! Now, tell me some stories!

(WIVES start telling a story as they ALL walk offstage; DIEDRICH remains)

ABOUT THE AUTHORS

AMANDA RUBY earned a BA (Edinboro University) and an MA (Kent State) in theatre. Over the years she has acted, directed, designed costumes, been a dramaturg, and taught theatre to college kids (whether they liked it or not). She created and runs an after-school theatre program at local Elementary and Middle schools called Acting Up! Amanda also enjoys producing plays for her local community theatre. When she isn't at a school or theatre, she really loves being at home with her two kids and husband.

BRENDAN P. KELSO came to writing modified Shakespeare scripts when he was taking time off from work to be at home with his newly born son. "It just grew from there". Within months, he was being asked to offer classes in various locations and acting organizations along the Central Coast of California. Originally employed as an engineer, Brendan never thought about writing. However, his unique personality, humor, and love for engaging the kids with The Bard has led him to leave the engineering world and pursue writing as a new adventure in life! He has always believed, "the best way to learn is to have fun!" Brendan makes his home on the Central Coast of California and loves to spend time with his wife and kids.

CAST AUTOGRAPHS

www.ingramcontent.com/pod-product-compliance
Lightning Source LLC
Chambersburg PA
CBHW060820050426
42449CB00008B/1746